Dividend Reinvestment Programs

By Patrick J. Davey

A Research Report from The Conference Board's Division of Management Research
Harold Stieglitz, Vice President

Contents

Tables

Charts

Exhibits

Foreword

UNTIL FAIRLY RECENTLY, the automatic reinvestment of dividends was only an idea whose time had not come. Now the situation is different; the concept has become a reality and a good many companies offer their shareholders dividend reinvestment programs.

Early in 1973, when they were in their early stages of development, The Conference Board published an article to help corporate executives assess the advantages and pitfalls of their programs.[1] Because much has happened in the development since then, the Board thought it appropriate to update and augment its earlier findings on reinvestment practices. This report is the result. Besides explaining why some companies offer reinvestment programs and others do not, it spells out the objectives that sponsors establish for their plans and indicates the extent to which these objectives have been attained. In addition, the report examines how companies organize and administer reinvestment programs. And it also contains participants' views on what the future holds for these arrangements.

The report should be useful to financial executives and others charged with responsibility for administering reinvestment programs, enabling them to compare their existing plans with those in other firms. It should also offer guidance to executives considering installation of such programs, since it describes the several varieties in use.

Other members of top management and even directors may find the report helpful because it provides insights into the experience and opinions of their peers on such important matters as cost allocations and administrative approaches. Bankers, brokers, investors and legislators should, too, because of their special interest in the evolution of reinvestment programs.

The Conference Board is indebted to the 143 corporate executives and two bankers who provided information for this

[1] Francis J. Walsh, Jr. and Patrick J. Davey, "Automatic Dividend Reinvestment Programs," The Conference Board RECORD, February, 1973.

project. The research was conducted and the report written by Patrick J. Davey of the Board's Financial Management Research Staff.

DAVID G. MOORE
Executive Vice President,
Research

1.
Introduction

PRIOR TO 1968, formal arrangements permitting shareowners to increase their ownership participations in corporations through automatic reinvestment of their dividends were unknown. Now, less than a decade later, many publicly owned companies have considered dividend reinvestment programs and have either implemented or rejected them. And some early sponsors have already substantially revised their original plans to take advantage of innovations.

Since First National City Bank of New York (now Citibank) introduced the concept eight years ago, dividend reinvestment programs have proliferated. At the end of 1972, the *Wall Street Journal* estimated that 200 companies offered such arrangements. Georgeson & Co., an investor relations firm, placed the number of sponsors at 655 at the outset of 1976 and forecast that it could approach 1,000 by the end of 1977. But some companies after weighing the pros and cons of reinvestment plans have decided not to install them, at least for the present.

While stockholders have always had the right to receive their dividends and then use them to acquire additional shares, impediments of one kind or another have dissuaded some, particularly those with relatively few shares, from following this path. For one thing, the limited amounts of cash dividends received by some shareholders have made the purchase of whole shares impossible. For another, high commission fees have discouraged purchases in small dollar amounts (even when brokers could be found to handle such transactions). But the emergence of dividend reinvestment plans has removed these and similar hindrances and has made the reinvestment process practical, as well as reasonable, for the small investor. Indeed, although precise data are not available, indications are that currently stockholders participating in reinvestment programs number at least in the hundreds of thousands and make annual reinvestments amounting in the aggregate to not less than several hundred million dollars.

Dividend reinvestment programs, as will be seen, appear in several different formats. They also carry a variety of names; for

Table 1: Classification of Respondents by Industries

	Number of Respondents	Offer Reinvestment Plans		Percent Offering Reinvestment Programs
		Yes	No	
Manufacturing				
Aircraft and parts	5	4	1	
Blast furnaces, steel mills, rolling mills	6	4	2	
Chemicals, paints and allied products	5	4	1	
Construction materials	4	3	1	
Electrical machinery, equipment and supplies	5	2	3	
Ethical and proprietary drugs	6	5	1	
Food and kindred products	11	8	3	
Machinery and equipment	12	7	5	
Miscellaneous consumer products	7	4	3	
Miscellaneous industrial products	5	5		
Motor vehicles, parts and equipment	4	4		
Nonferrous metals	1	1		
Office, computing and accounting equipment	5	2	3	
Paper and allied products	5	5		
Petroleum products	7	4	3	
Rubber and miscellaneous plastic products	6	5	1	
Textiles and related products	2		2	
Total manufacturing	96	67	29	70

Table 1: Classification of Respondents by Industries (continued)

	Number of Respondents	Offer Reinvestment Plans		Percent Offering Reinvestment Programs
		Yes	No	
Nonmanufacturing				
Communication	5	3	2	
Electric and gas utilities	38	27	11	
Mining	2	1	1	
Transportation	1	1		
Wholesale and retail trade	1	1		
Total nonmanufacturing	47	33	14	70
Total companies	143	100	43	70

example, "Automatic Dividend Reinvestment," "Systematic Investment Service," "Dividend Investment Plan," and "Stockholders' Investment Service." But all reinvestment arrangements, at a minimum, offer corporate shareholders the opportunity easily to reinvest their dividends (regardless of amounts) in full or partial shares of sponsors' common stock at prevailing market prices. No effort beyond that expended to sign and return an authorization form is required of shareholders desiring to enroll in any such program.

Several recent developments — the utilization of reinvestment programs as capital-raising mechanisms, the introduction of plans with special features, and the elimination in certain arrangements of some or all service charges to plan participants, for instance — have attracted the attention of both corporate executives and individual investors. Their interest has prompted them to raise questions such as these:

- What benefits do corporations hope to gain by installing or revising reinvestment programs?What are the pluses and minuses for shareowners? Do reinvestment plans actually accomplish their objectives?
- Why have some companies refrained from establishing reinvestment arrangements? Under what circumstances might they reconsider their decisions?
- What kinds of reinvestment programs are corporations presently offering? How are companies apportioning the service costs of their programs?
- Who administers these arrangements? What problems, if any, have arisen from reinvestment activities? How have they been resolved?
- How do executives view the future for reinvestment programs?

Aim of This Report

This report explores answers to these and related questions given by firms that have dividend reinvestment programs and by firms that have considered but decided not to institute them. By examining the responses of the two groups it seeks to provide a compact reference source on current management attitudes, practices and outlooks with regard to dividend reinvestment arrangements.

Profile of Participants

The 143 contributors to this survey represent a broad cross section of the business community. Approximately two-thirds (96) are manufacturing companies; the remaining one-third (47), nonmanufacturing companies. All are largely publicly owned concerns whose shares trade on an exchange or in the over-the-counter market.

Besides furnishing written responses, a few participating companies also elaborated on their replies in interviews. Officers of two banks that serve as reinvestment program agents also contributed their perspectives.

In addition to affording an indication of the incidence of reinvestment programs Table 1 (pages 2-3) presents a classification, by industry, of the corporations furnishing replies. It shows virtually identical prevalence of dividend reinvestment programs for manufacturing and nonmanufacturing respondents.

2.
Corporate Postures on Reinvestment Programs

THIS CHAPTER HAS a fourfold purpose: to examine the objectives of the 100 participants that have launched reinvestment programs; to appraise the extent to which these objectives have been attained; to explore the rationale of the 43 participants that have thus far shied away from reinvestment programs; and to determine what circumstances might cause these firms to reconsider their positions. Executives of companies contemplating the installation or revision of dividend reinvestment programs may find this exposition helpful in their own decision making.

Objectives of Reinvestment Programs

Participating sponsors set five principal objectives for their reinvestment programs. While the improvement of shareholder relationships predominates, as the frequency tabulation below indicates, other objectives are also important to some companies. For example, organizations requiring regular infusions of capital sometimes install reinvestment programs to assist their financing efforts.

Objectives of Reinvestment Programs	*Number of Mentions*
Improving shareholder relationships	79
Stabilizing the stockholder base	26
Increasing market support for shares	20
Raising equity capital	12
Reducing costs	6

Improving Shareholder Relationships

Prompted by suggestions from stockholders, banks, consultants and management executives, or by the pressures created when competitors sponsor plans, companies launch reinvestment arrangements to bolster existing investor relations programs. These concerns hope to reap the goodwill of their stockholders by providing them with valuable investment services. (Details on the nature and costs of various arrangements are spelled out in Chapter 3.)

Although reinvestment programs, where offered, are available to both individual and institutional investors, it is the small or individual investors — the purchasers of from a few to several hundred shares of stock — to whom these arrangements are primarily directed. Reinvestment plans hold little appeal for institutional investors; unlike many individual stockholders, they already obtain the advantages of negotiated brokerage rates because of the customarily large amounts of their purchases.

The secretary and assistant general counsel of an electrical equipment manufacturer comments: "We concluded that dividend reinvestment would increase demand for the company stock by making it easier for the odd-lot investor to invest . . . and would lead to better shareholder relations by offering the shareholder a means of increasing his investment conveniently and at an expense considerably less than a broker's fees on odd-lot purchases."

Small stockholders are said to obtain numerous advantages through participation in reinvestment programs. Among them: reduced commissions rates; custodial and record-keeping services at low fees; full utilization of funds committed to programs through fractional share ownership; and the benefits of a dollar cost-averaging investment system. Here is how the explanatory brochure of a diversified manufactruring company puts the case for plan membership to its stockholders:

"Dividends are deposited directly with [the bank administrator], resulting in faster reinvestment, with the benefits of an automatic savings plan.

"Your investment builds upon itself like compound interest in a savings account because your increased holdings will generate additional dividend income which, in turn, will be reinvested.

"Your dividends are utilized on a total basis, due to crediting of fractional shares to your account.

"You are given the opportunity to add to your dividend reinvestment through voluntary additional cash investments.

"Through large lot stock purchases, your proportionate share of brokerage commissions is much lower than if you had bought your own shares in odd lots.

"Dollar cost averaging through regular and consistent stock purchases produces long-range benefits.

"Personal record keeping is simplified. You receive detailed account statements from the bank promptly after each dividend reinvestment.

"You maintain voting control of your shares.

"You may join at any time or terminate at any time."

Stabilizing the Stockholder Base

For various reasons, such as protection against takeover, many corporations prefer widespread ownership of their shares. These companies often inaugurate reinvestment plans to help achieve this end. They believe the mere existence of a reinvestment program, because of its cost attractiveness, serves as a constant beacon wooing new individual investors. And they think shareholders who enroll in these arrangements are more likely to retain their shares — a tendency that reinvestment sponsors desiring to avoid inordinate institutional ownership of shares favor. For example, the assistant secretary of an equipment manufacturer, in recounting the objectives of her company's reinvestment program, states: "We wanted to encourage individual shareholders to add to their investment in our stock, to encourage long-term holdings, and to attract new individual holders."

Increasing Market Support

Disturbed by the volatility that they believe institutional trading can cause, some sponsors introduce reinvestment programs in attempts to moderate wide swings in the prices of their shares. They think that the quarterly or more frequent purchases of large blocks of stock by program administrators create incremental demands for their shares and thus provide at least a modicum of support for market prices.

Raising Equity Capital

"Adoption of the plan . . . was proposed as a means of regularly receiving additional funds for the company's continuing construction program," explains the vice president and treasurer of a utility. Eleven other respondents — ten utilities and one manufacturer — that have discerned ongoing needs for equity capital also rely on reinvestment programs to raise portions of their capital requirements. Simply by using authorized but previously unissued shares in connection with reinvestment plans these companies obtain regular cash inflows, thereby reducing their dependence on other external financing sources. Under the more conventional approach, reinvestment demand is satisfied through already outstanding shares with sponsors receiving no direct financing support.

Reinvestment plans utilizing original shares can make important financing contributions to companies desiring to raise capital through regular equity additions. Various publications indicate, for instance, that the American Telephone and Telegraph Company raised $327 million in equity capital during 1975 through its reinvestment program.[1]

Reducing Costs

For several sponsors another reinvestment program objective, though usually a subordinate one, is reducing administrative expenses. These companies aim to obtain at least some cost savings by preparing and mailing fewer dividend checks and stock certificates. For example, an office equiment company executive says: "Although there are some very small savings to the company (i.e., postage for all the dividends that would have to be sent . . .), the major benefit was that we were able to provide a shareholder service and accommodation that was worthwhile and appropriate."

Degrees of Success of Reinvestment Programs

Determining whether and to what degree reinvestment programs are successful poses problems for many companies. To begin with, most companies state objectives in qualitative terms — improving shareholder relations, for instance — a condition that makes precise measurement impossible. Then, too, many programs have multiple objectives. As a result, if conclusions on the achievement of individual goals differ, judgment of overall program worth is anything but easy. Nevertheless, participating sponsors have provided impressions on the extent to which they believe reinvestment programs have fulfilled their expectations. These conclusions on program accomplishments are categorized in the following tabulation:

[1]"Gaining Favor: A Way to Plow Back Dividends," *U.S. News & World Report,* May 24, 1976, p. 79.

Sponsors' Judgments on Their Programs' Accomplishments	*Number of Companies*
Exceeded expectations	2
Satisfied with results	45
Partly satisfied with results	28
Disappointed with results	8
Uncertain	5
Not indicated	12
Total	100

In all cases where sponsors assess the relative success of programs, the level of stockholder participation is the basic denominator. Both companies in which results outpaced expectations include the raising of equity capital among their programs' objectives. And those satisfied — as well as those dissatisfied — with accomplishments base their determinations largely on subjective conclusions as to how the percentage of eligible stockholders who participate contrasts with the percentage of those that do not; participation levels are not, as a rule, measured against norms. Respondents evincing only partial satisfaction with results are, for the most part, pleased with the operations of their programs, but disapponted with the numbers of enrollments by shareowners. Those uncertain about the success of their programs have launched them within the past year or so and have too little experience to express opinions.

Levels of Participation

Stockholder participation in reinvestment programs among 93 companies providing this information ranges from a low of 1.4 percent to a high of 19.5 percent; the median is 6.3 percent (Chart 1). Included in the preceding figures are participation statistics from 10 of the 14 contributing concerns that absorb service and brokerage charges in connection with their reinvestment programs. In these companies stockholder participation levels range from 6.5 percent to 19.5 percent; the median is 11 percent.

Five companies providing details on membership levels in reinvestment programs also volunteered information on the extent of participants' stockholdings. The percentage of outstanding

Chart 1: Stockholder Participation in 93 Reinvestment Programs

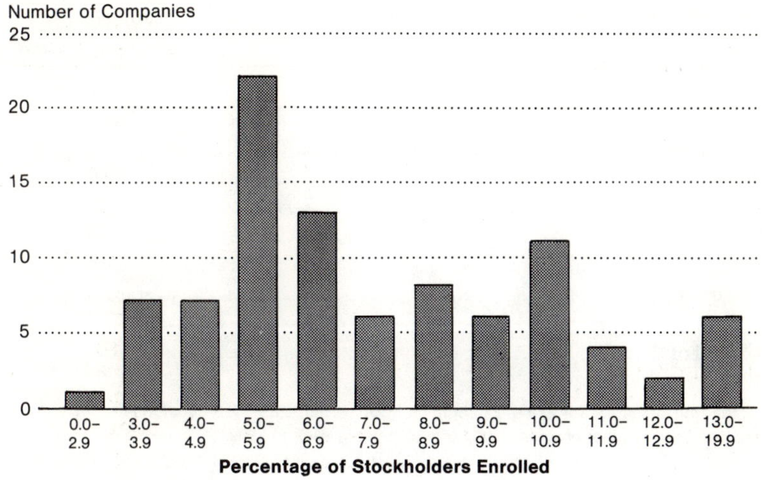

shares owned by these plan members is lower in all cases (typically by about half) than the percentage of total stockholders they constitute. In one company, for example, 3.26 percent of outstanding shares are owned by the 7.3 percent of stockholders enrolled in the dividend reinvestment plan.

Participation Trends

Most contributing companies started their reinvestment programs a year or more ago (see Table 2). Sufficient time has elapsed to enable many of them to determine trends in stockholder participation. These trends are outlined in the tabulation below:

Participation Trend	*Number of Companies*
Higher	67
Static	17
Lower	5
Too soon to know or not stated	11
Total	100

Table 2: Reinvestment Program Starting Dates in 100 Participating Companies

*Year**	*Number of Programs Started*
1970	1
1971	5
1972	20
1973	39
1974	18
1975	14
Not indicated	3
Total	100

*Starting dates are for existing programs; four participants have substantially revised or replaced their original programs, one of which dated back to 1969.

What accounts for the gains in stockholder participation that the majority of participating firms with reinvestment programs have achieved? Among the explanations offered by respondents:

• Active resolicitation of existing shareowners — Some sponsors use a variety of approaches to encourage participation. These include special annual follow-up mailings to stockholders and the inclusion of reminders in interim and annual reports on the existence and advantages of programs.

• General publicity given all such programs — Broad press coverage afforded reinvestment programs encourages participation, in the view of some. So, according to others, does the growing number of brochures describing reinvestment that are distributed to stockholders as the number of companies offering programs increases.

• Solicitation of all new stockholders — A number of reinvestment sponsors make a point of contacting all new stockholders to advise them of the program's availability. This practice, they believe, produces net membership increments.

• Plan improvements and cost reductions — A few sponsors that either have added to the options available under their original programs or that have absorbed some or all of the costs formerly passed along to participants recorded especially noteworthy gains in participation. They associate the increased enrollments with these plan modifications.

What about companies where participation levels have remained fairly constant or dropped? A common characteristic of their programs is that promotional efforts seem not to have been stressed. Additionally, a food company that experienced a sharp decline in stockholder participation explains that many former participating shareholders took capital gains following a sharp run-up in the price of its shares. It expects to launch a new campaign shortly in an attempt to increase participation. Another company reporting a falloff in the percentage of shareowners enrolled indicates that the absolute number of shareholders participating has increased slightly since the inception of its plan but not in sufficient amount to balance the growth in total shareholders.

Reinvestment Programs Not for All

Forty-three of those providing their experiences for this survey have decided to forego, at least for the time being, dividend reinvestment programs. These companies share two characteristics with the 100 participants that have implemented reinvestment programs: they are in the same industries and they are of large size. Furthermore, the objectives of reinvestment sponsors, with the possible exception of raising equity capital, appeal to many nonofferers of dividend reinvestment programs.

But, despite these similarities, there are also significant differences between the groups. These differences — in management philosophies and dividend policies, for instance — are responsible for the division of postures on reinvestment.

Respondents that have considered and rejected dividend reinvestment programs offer a variety of explanations for their conclusions. These reasons, listed in order of frequency of mention, relate to:

- Dividend payouts
- Anticipated participation levels
- Cost considerations
- Ownership profiles

- Possible adverse effects
- Philosophical objections

Dividend Payouts

Several companies point out their cash dividends are low in relation to the prices for which their shares customarily trade. This circumstance makes the implementation of a reinvestment plan impractical; too long a time period is required to enable participating shareholders to acquire significant amounts of stock. Assume, for the purpose of illustration, that a company with shares trading in the range $120 to $140 pays a quarterly cash dividend of $1 a share and offers a reinvestment program. The owner of 20 shares of stock in the company would, as a reinvestment program participant, require more than a year of dividend plowbacks to add a single share to his holdings — a lag likely to deter enrollment.

Other dividend payment practices that constrain participants from putting reinvestment programs into effect include: payment of cash dividends at irregular intervals or in diminished amounts; emphasizing stock distributions in dividend policies; and, of course, interruption in the payment of cash dividends.

Anticipated Participation Levels

About a dozen participants decided not to institute reinvestment programs after reviewing projections on the percentages of shareholders that would enroll. These forecasts — based on surveys of stockholders in a few cases, observations of participation levels elsewhere in others, and examinations of shareholder inquiries in still others — led the companies to believe that too few stockholders would enroll to make reinvestment programs worthwhile.

A food company, for instance, that refused to install a reinvestment program blames expected poor enrollment for the rejection. Its vice president-finance and treasurer explains: "The reason we have not adopted a program to date is our impression that the level of participation is typically quite low. Indications we have received suggest that substantially fewer than 10 percent of stockholders participate and this invariably translates into a much smaller percentage of total shares outstanding because the program is most popular with the smaller stockholders."

Cost Considerations

"Our company has examined several different proposals for dividend reinvestment and has concluded that the cost is not justified by the benefits to the individual stockholder or to the corporation." This statement by the vice president of a utility is typical of the comments made by participating executives whose concerns hesitate to implement reinvestment programs because they conclude start-up and maintenance costs outweigh advantages.

Others believe it would be necessary to make significant outlays continually to ensure the survival of programs and they decline to sanction such financial drains. And a few respondents think that company expenditures on reinvestment programs discriminate against nonparticipants.

Ownership Profiles

A small number of companies whose stockholder lists are dominated by institutional holders think reinvestment programs are inappropriate, especially since they wish to retain existing ownership profiles. Others, unconcerned by the makeup of shareowners rolls, opine they have too few individual investors to make a program feasible. And one company, unlike its many counterparts that install dividend reinvestment programs to encourage broadened investment by individuals, fears the implementation of a reinvestment program would result in an unwanted concentration of share ownership.

Possible Adverse Effects

Several respondents believe that, rather than improving investor relations, dividend reinvestment programs impair them. These companies maintain that most of their stockholders need to receive cash dividends. Reinvestment programs, in their views, not only cause misunderstandings about the tax obligations that attach to reinvested dividends but also remove the wherewithal certain stockholders require to discharge these liabilities. And a few hold dividend reinvestment programs are nuisances that invite legal hassles, including possible confrontations with the Securities and Exchange Commission (SEC) over registration statements or other matters.

Philosophical Objections

Two polled executives voice fundamental objections to reinvestment plans. One feels these arrangements mislead individual investors by encouraging them to place more importance on income than on growth in making stock selections. The other, a communications company vice president and treasurer, believing all these programs have inherent flaws, expresses his opposition this way:

> "It is our philosophical point of view that any program which induces investment in a stock regardless of its price is fundamentally unsound, and ought not to be encouraged."

Posture Change Possibilities

Eight of the forty-three respondents that presently do not have dividend reinvestment programs are reconsidering their positions, and five of these companies indicate they will probably soon implement such arrangements. Eight others do not foresee any developments that might cause them to alter their decisions on reinvestment programs. But many of the remaining 27 firms envisage circumstances under which they might institute reinvestment programs. These include: significant expansions of interest on the part of stockholders, tight equity markets over prolonged periods, improved operating results permitting the payment of cash dividends, switches to cash payments from stock distributions in dividend policies, and tax law revisions granting relief to stockholders reinvesting dividends. For example, the assistant treasurer of a steel company says:

> "Our dividend reinvestment file dates from 1968, and we review our position regularly. Our quarterly reports have asked our shareholders to indicate their interest in dividend reinvestment. If our shareholders should show a greater interest, or if the percentage participation should increase for similar plans, we would certainly reconsider dividend reinvestment."

3.
Organizing for Reinvestment

PLANNING FOR DIVIDEND reinvestment programs — sometimes done by the sponsor alone but often accomplished with the assistance of banks or investor relations firms — concentrates on four areas: (1) development of strategies; (2) cost considerations; (3) communications with investors; and (4) program administration. Practices with regard to the first three are examined in this chapter; discussion of administrative aspects is reserved for Chapter 4.

Reinvestment Strategies

What kind of reinvestment plan is most suitable? What type of shares — original or outstanding — shall be used? Who shall be eligible for participation? These are the basic questions corporations must grapple with in planning their reinvestment arrangements.

Types of Reinvestment Plans

A few years ago, companies attempting to facilitate increased equity ownership by investors did not exercise discretion in selecting the type of reinvestment plan to implement or the type of shares to use. All these sponsors picked simple dividend reinvestment plans employing outstanding shares because of the ready availability of such arrangements and because alternatives were still on the drawing board. Today, as a result of the rapid evolution of the dividend reinvestment concept, companies considering the implementation of a reinvestment program are less confined. They have three basic arrangements from which to choose: (1) simple dividend reinvestment plans; (2) dividend reinvestment plus optional cash contributions plans; and (3) combination plans, under which dividend reinvestment is a right but not a requirement of participation. In addition, sponsors presently decide whether to use outstanding or original shares in filling reinvestment demand. Chart 2 reflects participants' preferences in both regards.

Chart 2: Reinvestment Programs in 100 Participating Companies

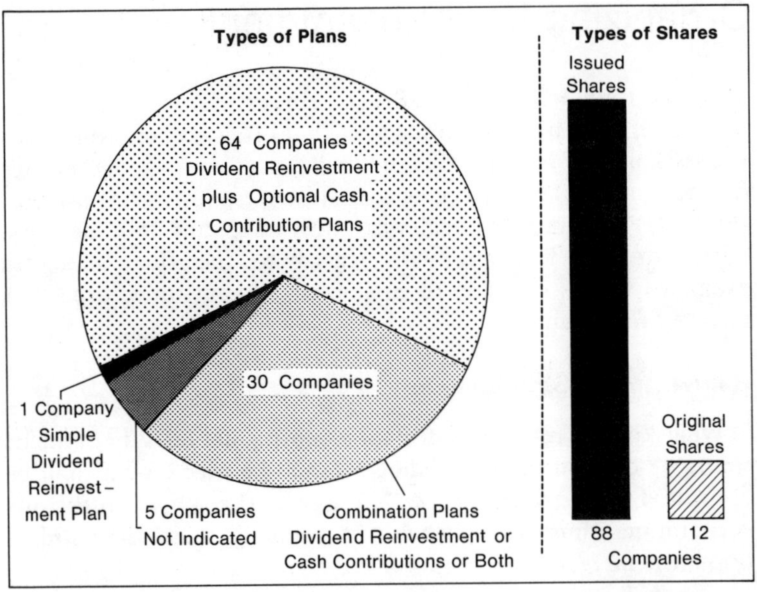

Simple Dividend Reinvestment Plans

Simple dividend reinvestment plans — only one of which is still in use among survey respondents — form the basis of all present-day reinvestment programs. Shareholders who enroll in this type of arrangement agree to have their cash dividends paid to an agent, rather than receive them in the usual way. The agent, in turn, uses the aggregated dividends of individual members to purchase blocks of shares in the dividend-paying corporation on their behalf.

Dividend Reinvestment Plus Optional Cash Contribution Plans

A majority of queried sponsors now utilize reinvestment arrangements that have simple dividend reinvestment as their foundation but which also offer plan participants an additional option: adding to their reinvestments by making supplementary cash contributions. Incorporating a voluntary cash payment feature, in the view of advocates, increases the attractiveness of reinvestment programs. Some shareholders who might not otherwise participate because of the limited number of shares simple dividend reinvestment would permit them to accumulate are encouraged to enroll. And other shareholders, who would be attracted by the advantages of simple dividend reinvestment, find their interest intensified because of the commission savings (illustrated in Exhibit 2, page 26) that attach to supplementary cash investments in the common shares of sponsoring companies.

Fifty-eight of the participants sponsoring dividend reinvestment plans that contain cash contribution options set ranges for the permissible amounts that may be invested in a period; the other six companies impose no constraints save for minimum amounts that may be contributed. These limitations are outlined in the following tabulation.

Limitations on Cash Contributions	*Number of Companies*
$10 to $1,000 monthly [1]	48
$50 to $1,000 quarterly	4
$10 to $1,000 quarterly [2]	2
$50 to $1,000 monthly	1
$25 to $1,000 monthly	1
$10 to $3,000 quarterly	1
$10 to $500 monthly	1
$10 and more without limit at any time [3]	4
$25 and more without limit	1
$10 to $1,000 from time to time	1
Total	64

[1] Cash payments must be in multiples of $10 in three plans.

[2] Cash payments must be in multiples of $10 in one plan.

[3] Cash payments must be in multiples of $10 in all plans.

Combination Plans

Thirty respondents sponsor combination reinvestment plans that afford enrolled investors three different ways of increasing their ownership participations: dividend reinvestment, cash contributions, or both. These combination arrangements differ from plans offering dividend reinvestment plus optional cash payments in that they do not make dividend reinvestment a precondition to the investment of cash contributions. Thus participants in these plans have the option of receiving their dividends in the usual manner, and still obtaining the advantages of adding to company holdings conveniently and at low cost. (In eight of the ten cases where information is available, dividends paid on the shares acquired by participants exercising only the cash payment option of these plans are automatically reinvested.) Of course, members of combination plans may, if they so elect, reinvest their dividends and also make supplementary cash contributions.

Proponents of combination type reinvestment plans find them attractive because, unlike other plans with cash contribution features, they do not preclude from membership shareholders who want to receive dividends in the usual way. However, participants in these arrangements are subject, as the following tabulation indicates, to limitations on the timing and amount of cash contributions that resemble those imposed in other programs.

Limitation on Cash Contributions[1]	*Number of Companies*
$25 to $1,000 monthly	17
Maximum of $3,000 quarterly	4
$25 to $3,000 quarterly	2
$25 to $1,000 quarterly	2
$25 to $2,500 monthly	1
$20 to $1,000 monthly	1
$10 to $1,000 monthly	1
$25 to $500 quarterly	1
Maximum of $1,000 quarterly	1
Total	30

[1] Five companies require investors participating solely in the cash contribution segment of their reinvestment plans to make a minimum of four annual investments.

Original or Outstanding Shares?

As previously indicated, twelve participants issue original shares in connection with their reinvestment arrangements; the remaining eighty-eight rely on shares already outstanding. All twelve respondents that issue new shares to fill reinvestment demand sponsor combination-type reinvestment plans.

Original issue plans have special appeal to capital-intensive companies because they provide a convenient means not only of improving stockholder relationships but also of obtaining at least a portion of financing requirements. In addition, by providing equity inflows these arrangements benefit concerns striving to restore balance to capital structures that are heavily debt laden.

To issue original shares companies must first obtain permission from the SEC. This involves the filing of registration statements — documents that contain comprehensive background and financial particulars about the companies — with that body. Prospectuses summarizing the details contained in registration statements and describing the operations of reinvestment plans must then be made available to eligible investors by sponsors. The appendix consists of a case study that examines the development, objectives, achievements and administration of a participating utility's original-share reinvestment program.

Of course, the eighty-eight participants that rely on outstanding shares to satisfy reinvestment needs do not number raising funds among the objectives of their reinvestment programs. These firms either have doubts about using reinvestment programs in financing roles, seldom require external financing, or prefer always to turn to other sources — investment and commercial banks, for example — to meet capital needs. There are other reasons adduced for choosing outstanding shares over original shares. One is avoidance of the registration process. Another is fear of dilution that can occur if the market price of shares falls below the book value, or if per share earnings decline.

Eligibility

Regardless of the types of reinvestment programs they offer, all sponsors open them to all their common stockholders — the individual and institutional recipients of dividend payments. A dozen of these concerns also invite their preference or preferred shareholders to participate. And four that restrict plan memberships to holders of common shares arrange, if requested, to reinvest any dividends or interest payments these shareowners receive from their investments in other of the sponsoring companies' securities

— preferred shares or bonds — as optional cash contributions.

A few companies take care to warn their shareowning top executives of the possible perils of reinvestment program participation. These officials are subject to provisions of the Securities Exchange Act of 1934 that deal with reporting changes in ownership interests and realization of "short swing" profits. Although this law does not absolutely prohibit participation in dividend reinvestment plans by such executives, it causes some companies to caution them against membership. "We have advised insiders — primarily officers and directors — not to participate because of possible technical security law violations as a result of the 'automatic' nature of purchase timing," says the treasurer and controller of a food company, for example.

While eligibility requirements vary somewhat among plan sponsors, participation is always entirely voluntary. Normally, an investor desiring to participate must agree to reinvest the full amount of the dividend. However, several sponsors have made arrangements that permit investors to receive portions of their dividends and still remain eligible for participation. In these instances sponsors maintain two separate accounts in an investor's name, one participating in the reinvestment plan and the other not.

Like participation, withdrawal from plan membership is entirely voluntary; the investor need only inform the sponsor or plan administrator of the desire to discontinue membership. Thereafter dividends are directly paid in the regular way. Of course, an investor can also bring participation in a reinvestment program to a close by selling the shares owned in the sponsoring firm.

Cost Allocations

Two general kinds of costs attach to the operation of dividend reinvestment programs: those incurred in their implementation and maintenance, and those connected with their related investment activities. Sponsors always absorb the former, but only occasionally the latter.

Organization and Maintenance Costs

Printing and mailing expenses are among the principal costs related to the organization and maintenance of reinvestment programs. Announcement letters, authorization cards, and descriptive brochures must be prepared and mailed to all eligible investors at the time plans are launched. Such material (or revised versions if plans are modified) must also be used for resolicitations as well as for notifications to new shareholders.

Other costs incurred by sponsors include those for correspondence and programming. While correspondence costs primarily relate to the preparation and delivery of status reports to plan participants, they also arise in connection with communications responding to inquiries or acknowledging enrollments and contributions.

Offsetting, to varying degrees, the organization and maintenance costs experienced by sponsors are the savings derived from the processing and mailing of fewer dividend checks and stock certificates. Although net costs fluctuate from company to company, depending on such factors as the number of shareholders contacted, some indication of their amounts may be obtained from the schedules of a participating utility (see Exhibit 1, page 24).

Service and Brokerage Costs

Investment-related expenses of reinvestment programs arise from two sources: service charges imposed by administrators for keeping records and acting as custodians for acquired shares, and commissions levied by brokers for handling securities transactions. When it comes to allocating these costs, sponsors can totally absorb both charges, fully absorb either charge, partially absorb either or both charges, or pass through the charges in their entirety to plan members.

Fourteen of the 96 companies providing information on the handling of service and brokerage costs fully absorb them; the remainder (82), to an unspecified but in most cases seemingly complete extent, pass them along to shareholders enrolled in their reinvestment programs. The 14 respondents that absorb all costs include the 12 firms that issue original shares to satisfy reinvestment demand. (In effect, these sponsors are assuming only service charges because no brokerage is involved in the distribution of authorized but previously unissued stock.)

Service fees, when charged to individual program participants by administrators, are assessed each time reinvestments are made on their behalf. Typically, they are fixed percentages of the amounts invested (dividends and/or optional cash contributions) up to a specified dollar ceiling. Only rarely are service charges flat amounts

Exhibit 1: Reinvestment Program Costs and Savings — A Utility Company

Cost to Implement Service

Description	*Cost*
Cost to print 50,000 brochures	$1,300
Cost to print 50,000 authorization cards and letters	600
Cost to mail 48,000 brochures	6,000
Cost to convert data processing	1,500
Total cost to implement service	$9,400

Annual Cost to Solicit the New Shareholders

Description	*Cost*
Cost of 5,000 brochures	$350
Cost to mail 5,000 brochures	550
Total cost to notify new shareholders	$900

Annual Confirmation Expenses

Description	*Cost*
Mailing of quarterly confirmation	$2,040
Total service charge	$2,040
Total costs	$12,340

Annual Cost Savings to Print and Process Fewer Checks

Description	*Cost*
Costs for checks	$ 160
Cost to process checks	35
Cost to mail checks	1,200
Total cost savings	$1,395

Table 3: Service Charges Assessed Reinvestment Program Members

Service Charge per Investment [1]	*Number of Programs*
5% to maximum of $2.50	53
5% to maximum of $3.00	3
5% to maximum of $2.00	2
4% to maximum of $2.50	15
4% to maximum of $2.00	1
4% to maximum of $1.50	1
2% to maximum of $2.00	3
5% on reinvested dividend amount (minimum $.50, maximum $3.00); 5% on cash contributions (minimum $1.25, maximum $3.00)	1
5% on reinvested dividend amount (minimum $1.25, maximum $3.00)	1
5% on reinvested dividend amount (minimum $1.00, maximum $5.00); $3.00 on cash contributions	1
5% on reinvested dividends amount to maximum $3.00; $3.00 on cash contributions	1
$2.00 on reinvested dividend amount; $3.00 on cash contributions	1
No charge	14
Not indicated	3
Total	100

[1] Except where otherwise indicated, service charges are assessed on the amounts invested regardless of whether they consist of dividends, cash contributions, or combinations of both.

or do they depend on whether dividends or optional cash contributions are being invested (see Table 3).

Reinvestment plan participants who bear service costs also have to pay proportionate shares of brokerage commissions. However, because bulk purchasing by administrators keeps these fees low — usually less than 2 percent of the amount of dividends, cash payments, or combinations of dividends and cash payments invested — they serve as inducements rather than deterrents to plan memberships. Exhibit 2 (page 26), a tabulation from a brochure describing the reinvestment program of a participating manufacturer, shows why this is so.

Exhibit 2: Reinvestment Program Service Charges and Estimated Brokerage Commissions — A Manufacturing Company

(1) Quarterly Dividends[1]	(2) Bank Service Charge	(3) Brokerage Commission (assume 1%)	(4) Total Acquisition Cost (2) + (3)	(5) Estimated Cost of Investing Same Amount through Broker	(6) Indicated Savings (5)—(4)
$ 5.00	$ .50	$ .05	$ .55	May Not Handle	
10.00	.50	.10	.60	May Not Handle	
25.00	1.00	.20	1.20	May Not Handle	
25.00	1.25	.25	1.50	$ 6.90	$ 5.40
50.00	2.50	.50	3.00	7.40	4.40
75.00	2.50	.75	3.25	7.90	4.65
100.00	2.50	1.00	3.50	8.40	4.90
200.00	2.50	2.00	4.50	10.40	5.90
500.00	2.50	5.00	7.50	14.40	6.90
1000.00	2.50	10.00	12.50	25.00	12.50

[1] May include optional cash payments. If additional amounts are invested under the Optional Cash Investment feature, the amount in column (1) will equal the amount of dividend plus voluntary cash payment.

Another one-time cost, evidently always borne by the plan participant, is the expense that attaches to the termination of plan membership on a cash-settlement basis. Charges assessed under respondents' programs are outlined in Table 4. If the withdrawing member merely ceases his participation in the reinvestment program while retaining his stock interest in the company, he can usually obtain a certificate free of charge for the shares held in his name by the administrator.

Communications with Investors

Once preliminary details such as plan selection and cost allocations are resolved, sponsors have to apprise potential reinvestment program participants of their decisions. To do this most companies follow a fairly standard routine: They forward letters to their shareholders announcing the availability of plans and include explanatory brochures and enrollment cards. Of course, the format of such communications sometimes varies. For example, some companies, rather than mail three separate pieces of correspondence, use only two: a letter and a descriptive brochure that incorporates a tear-off authorization form. Other companies combine the announcement letter and explanatory material in a booklet and provide a separate authorization form.

Announcement Letters

Whether included in descriptive brochures or mailed separately, announcement letters are usually signed by either the chairman of

Table 4: Charges for Withdrawal from Reinvestment Programs

Withdrawal Charge	*Number of Programs*
$1 plus brokerage	59
Brokerage only	16
$2.50 plus brokerage	11
$2.00	2
Maximum of $2.50	1
Not indicated	11
Total	100

the board or the president of the sponsor, or both. The letters tend to be brief and narrowly focused. Besides offering membership, they may succinctly describe the advantages of the program. Many also suggest that recipients carefully review the explanatory literature before reaching a decision on enrollment.

Descriptive Brochures

Booklets on reinvestment programs provide investors with the detailed information they need to decide on participation. Some sponsors use brochures furnished by their administrators, while others assemble their own descriptive material. But regardless of how they are prepared, the brochures have the same objectives. They are designed to explain how membership benefits investors, what costs they will incur, how programs work, and what the conditions of participation are.

Sponsors that fill reinvestment demand with original shares issue prospectuses (or summaries of prospectuses) rather than descriptive booklets to describe their reinvestment programs. Prospectuses differ from standard explanatory brochures in several respects. For one thing, prospectuses are far more comprehensive; they include background and financial particulars on sponsors while standard brochures do not. For another, prospectuses usually employ the question-and-answer technique to explain programs whereas standard brochures tend, with few exceptions, to offer straight narrative presentations.

Authorization Forms

Authorization forms must be signed and returned to plan administrators if investors intend to participate in reinvestment programs. The signed cards authorize the sponsor to withhold direct payment of dividends to stockholders and to pay them to plan administrators instead. They may also permit administrators to enroll investors in the voluntary cash payment arrangements.

Other Contacts

Some companies send acknowledgement letters to stockholders who enroll in their reinvestment programs. And, as necessary, sponsors make telephone calls or write letters to respond to stockholders' questions on reinvestment programs.

A number of companies contact investors who acquire stock interests subsequent to the sending of reinvestment program announcements to make them aware of the programs' availability. And some undertake annual or occasional resolicitation efforts that require mailings similar to those used to launch programs. Other sponsors refer to their reinvestment programs in annual and interim reports and invite inquiries from interested investors.

4. Administration of Reinvestment Programs

COMPANIES THAT IMPLEMENT reinvestment programs must decide at the beginning the extent to which they wish to be involved in the administration of their arrangements. They may elect to manage the plans themselves, using banks in purchasing and custodial capacities when necessary. Or they may delegate administrative responsibilities to outsiders. Only six participants manage their own plans; the other 94 with reinvestment plans employ external administrators — namely, banks.

External Administration

Prominent among the reasons sponsors advance for turning to banks as administrators are:

• Lower cost — Many firms have banks administer their reinvestment plans because they find that farming out the job is less expensive than doing it in-house. Also, some believe that program costs should be borne entirely by participants and that external administration, in the words of an oil company executive, "forestalls escalation of absorption of plan costs by the company."

• Service capabilities — Most participants say they lacked the necessary know-how to provide proper service when they decided to install reinvestment plans. Rather than take the time and spend the money to train personnel and develop data processing techniques, these companies sought outside assistance. And because they were already using banks or banking affiliates to process their shareholder records, they simply availed themselves of the reinvestment services that these banks had already developed.

• Other considerations — Several sponsors that rely on banks to administer their plans are philosophically opposed to self-administration; they believe that investment activities should be completely divorced from normal business operations. Others that have chosen outsiders wish to prevent possible confrontations with the SEC. And one company employs a bank administrator "to avoid registration under the Securities Act of 1933, and to avoid restrictions on the company's ability to acquire treasury shares."

The following comments by respondents contain typical explanations on the use of outside reinvestment program administrators:

"We opted for external management of the program because otherwise there would have been a large duplication of effort as we attempted to administer one small part of our overall shareholder program while leaving the bulk of the administration to our transfer agent."

— *Chairman and president, a machinery company*

* * *

"Because a dividend reinvestment plan was a new idea to our company in 1973, we opted to have our program administered by an outside agency which was more familiar with this concept in shareholder service and better equipped to manage it."

— *Vice president and treasurer, a communications company*

* * *

"We chose an outside agent because of cost. We simply could not program and staff the program for the same money."

— *Assistant treasurer, a pharmaceutical company*

Selecting External Administrators

Choosing one bank from the many that offer reinvestment services is a basic responsibility of all sponsors that decide on external administration for their programs. While not an unusually difficult task, the choice of a bank administrator can prove time-consuming, especially if a large number of proposals are reviewed.

Among those polled, satisfaction with existing relationships most frequently accounts for the selection of a reinvestment program administrator. Participants pleased with the work banks perform for them as registrars, transfer agents, dividend disbursing agents or, in some cases, just as suppliers of loans often retain these same banks to manage their reinvestment plans.

Other respondents choose their administrators on the basis of experience. These companies employ banks that have pioneered in the development of reinvestment plans and that have fully demonstrated their managerial competence.

Still other survey participants find comparisons among the types of plans offered by potential administrators useful in the selection

How Dividend Reinvestment Programs Work

Plans that are self-administered or employ original shares aside, all dividend reinvestment programs operate in much the same way. Sponsoring companies prepare dividend checks on the basis of stockholder rolls but withhold payments to those investors that bank administrators indicate are program members. These unpaid dividends are aggregated and forwarded to banks which use them to purchase shares on the open market for plan members. Banks also amass supplementary cash contributions made by shareholders, under programs permitting them, for eventual reinvestment. Administrators hold the shares so acquired in custody and provide participants with appropriate reports.

Explanations of how individual programs work appear in the descriptive pamphlets or prospectuses that sponsors furnish investors. The following excerpt from the brochure of a construction materials company is representative:

"Upon receipt of your completed authorization form, the bank will open an account in your name. Future dividends and any

process. They have picked the banks whose approaches are most compatible with their own attitudes on reinvestment.

And in several cases ready accessibility is an important consideration in the selection of administrators. Sponsors influenced by a bank's location think that having an administrator close at hand facilitates coordination and control of their reinvestment programs.

A few respondents indicate that persistent solicitation by administrators resulted in their selection. In these instances, sponsors that were undecided on the implementation of reinvestment programs eventually accepted the services proffered by the banks that contacted them.

Internal Administration

Of the six respondents that administer their own investment programs, four are utilities that use original shares to fill reinvestment demand. The remaining two are manufacturers. One of these relies on issued and outstanding shares for reinvestment purposes; the other, on original shares. Three of the four utilities voluntary cash investments will be credited to your account after deduction of the service charge. The bank will combine funds received from all participants and make a bulk purchase of stock. Promptly after making the purchase, the bank will send each participant an itemized statement of amount received, service charge, shares purchased (full and fractional), cost of purchase, and new share balance.

"Cash dividends on shares purchased by the bank for your account are automatically used to purchase additional shares at no extra charge.

"You do nothing else. All future voluntary cash investments and dividend reinvestments will be promptly confirmed to you by the bank. To maintain your account, you need make only four investments a year, although you may make more at any time. The four investments may include both reinvested dividends and voluntary cash investments. If you make less than four investments in a year, the bank will notify you. But you will still have 30 days to make a new investment and keep your account active."

manage all aspects of their programs; the remaining utility coadministers its program with a bank. The manufacturing concern that employs outstanding shares for its reinvestment program serves as its own transfer agent and employs a bank to purchase shares and act as custodian for plan members. The other manufacturer completely self-administers its program.

At least three out of the six companies that now administer their own reinvestment programs formerly used outsiders (banks and in one case a broker) as managers. These sponsors switched to in-house management when they changed from issued to original share arrangements. The development of necessary computer skills permitted the changeovers; the pursuit of cost saving and more customized servicing of plan participants prompted them.

As for the industrial concern that acts as its own transfer agent, the primary motivation for self-administration is to gain experience in managing stockholder accounts when share certificates are not issued. The company's vice president and secretary elaborates:

"We consider dividend reinvestment plans as the preliminary step — or spearhead — toward establishment and widespread use of a transfer agent, custodian or depository system permitting stockholders to authorize retention of their stock certificates by the transfer agent (comparable to the mutual fund approach). Such a system offers substantial advantages to the issuer and to the average stockholder, leading, as it will in time, to acceptance of uncertificated stock."

Administrative Duties and Guidelines

All sponsors, of course, expect both bank and internal administrators to conform strictly with the procedures contained in the agreement sections of the booklets used to explain reinvestment plans. The procedures are fairly standard; basically, they call for administrators to: purchase shares on behalf of participants (where issued shares are used); provide custodial services for shares acquired by plan members; furnish record-keeping services; vote acquired shares in accordance with the owners' wishes; and be responsible to members' needs in related investment matters.

Administrators draw up the agreements that spell out their responsibilities in managing reinvestment programs for companies which sponsor them. The agreements, however, exist not between administrators and plan sponsors, but between administrators and individual plan members (see Exhibit 3, pages 36-39).

Some survey respondents make further explicit demands on their reinvestment program administrators; for example, accurate as well as prompt reporting to plan members and themselves; complete conformity with rules of the Securities and Exchange Commission (SEC) and stock exchanges in investment matters; and thorough responses to shareowners' inquiries and complaints. One participating company specifically bars its bank administrator from using the list of its plan members for any purpose, other than furnishing reinvestment service, without prior approval.

Other respondents, however, refuse to become enmeshed in administrative matters either out of fear of running afoul of SEC regulations, such as those that apply to the rendering of investment advice, or because of other unspecified legal worries. They maintain "arms-length" relationships with administrators. Representative of the explanations offered by these companies for their stances is the following comment by the treasurer of a paper company:

"Inasmuch as counsel recommended that, once the plan was established and approved, the trustee (administrator) should be left entirely free to administer it without formal or informal intervention by the company, we have not established any guidelines."

Problems and Solutions

Forty respondents indicate they have experienced problems — usually of a minor nature — in connection with the administration of their reinvestment programs. For the most part, these difficulties, which arose in internally as well as externally administered plans, started soon after plans were implemented and were quickly cleared up. However, in a few cases difficulties have persisted and efforts to resolve them continue. Whether behind them or stll unsolved, the problems faced by individual sponsors fall into one or more of the following categories:

- Inadvertent plan enrollments
- Communication breakdowns
- Record-keeping errors
- Broker complaints

Unintentional Participation

Confusion on the part of investors sometimes leads to their unintended participation in reinvestment programs. A number of participating sponsors report that some of their shareholders mistake the authorization cards mailed them at the time reinvestment programs are launched for proxy requests. They sign and return the forms, apparently without reading them. These stockholders, of course, subsequently become upset when dividend payment dates arrive but dividend checks do not.

Respondents try a number of tacks to combat such snags. Most redesign authorization cards. For example, some use multicolored cards and others imprint phrases like "Not a Proxy" in large letters on their authorization cards to lessen their resemblance to proxy solicitation forms. Others send letters acknowledging memberships in reinvestment plans as soon as signed authorization cards are received — a tactic they say eases recisions of inadvertent enrollments. Yet another solution to the problem is described in the statement by the vice president and treasurer of a utility:

"Our one recurring problem is that many shareholders return the authorization we send them when, in fact, they do not wish to reinvest their

Exhibit 3: Systematic Investment Service Agreement,

1. As agent for the shareholder (participant) Bradford Trust Company ("Bradford"), after deducting the charges for its services specified in Item 5 below,

(a) will apply all cash dividends on the shares of [the company's] Common Stock held by the participant and on any full shares or fractional interest in one share (to four decimal places) acquired by him through this Service (Dividend Reinvestment Plan), and/or

(b) will apply all cash payments of $25 to $1,000 (but not more than $1,000 in any one month) received from the participant for such purchase (Cash Payment Plan),

as the participant may elect, to the purchase of full and fractional shares of [the company's] Common Stock for the participant's account. Such purchases may be made on any securities exchange where such shares are traded, in the over-the-counter market, or in negotiated transactions, and may be on such terms as to price, delivery and otherwise as Bradford, in its sole discretion may determine.

2. In making purchases for the participant's account, Bradford may commingle the participant's dividends and cash payments with those of other participants. In the case of each purchase, the price at which Bradford shall be deemed to have acquired shares for the participant's account shall be the average price (including all costs of purchase except the service charge shown in Item 5 below) of all shares purchased by it for participants in the Service with their aggregate funds used for such purchase. Bradford may hold the shares of all participants together in its name or in the name of its nominee. Bradford shall have no responsibility as to the market value of [the company's] Common Stock acquired for the participant's account. Dividends and cash payments will be invested by Bradford no later than within 30 days after receipt except where such investment would violate Rule 10B-6 under the Securities Exchange Act of 1934 or other applicable provisions of

Bradford Trust Company

the Federal Securities laws. Participants' funds held by Bradford will not bear interest. A participant may withdraw his entire cash payment by written notice received by Bradford not less than 48 hours before such payment is to be invested. It is understood that, in any event, Bradford shall have no liability in connection with inability to purchase shares or the timing of any purchases.

3. Following each purchase, Bradford will send to each participant whose funds have been applied to such purchase an advice of transactions in his account since the last prior purchase for his account, including a statement showing the current shares in the account.

4. No certificates will be issued to the participant for shares in his account unless he so requests Bradford in writing or his account is terminated. On written request, Bradford will send the participant certificates for any full shares credited to his account. Such requests shall be handled by Bradford without charge to the participant. A separate request must be made each time a participant wants certificates. No certificate for a fractional share will be issued but under the Dividend Reinvestment Plan dividends on a fractional interest in a share will be credited to the participant's account.

5. The charge per account for Bradford's service will be 4% of the amount received (dividends or cash payments or both) for each purchase of stock for such account, with a maximum charge of $2.50 per purchase per account. Bradford may also charge for additional services performed at the request of the participant and not provided for herein.

6. It is understood that the reinvestment of dividends does not relieve the participant of any taxes which may be payable on such dividends. Bradford will report annually to each participant the amount of dividends credited to his account during the year.

7. Any shares held by Bradford for the participants' accounts will be voted in accordance with the participants' directions. If a

participant does not direct how he wishes shares voted, Bradford will not vote such shares.

8. A participant may terminate his account at any time by giving written notice of termination to Bradford, but any such notice received by Bradford after a dividend record date from a Dividend Reinvestment Plan participant shall not be effective until dividends paid for such record date have been credited to his account. Upon termination, a participant will receive a certificate for all full shares in his account unless he elects cash. If he elects cash, Bradford will sell such shares and send the net proceeds to him after a service charge of $2.50 and applicable brokerage commissions, providing the participant's signature on the written request is properly guaranteed by a bank. Bradford may terminate any participant's account at any time in its discretion. In any case, the participant will receive cash in lieu of any fractional interest in a share at the then current market value of [the company's] Common Stock.

If a participant, under the Dividend Reinvestment Plan, disposes of all shares registered in his name on the books of [the company], Bradford may in its discretion continue to invest the dividends on the shares in his account, until otherwise notified in writing by the participant.

9. It is understood that stock dividends or stock splits or proceeds of sale of stock purchase rights on [the company's] Common Stock applicable to shares belonging to the participant whether held in his account or in his own name, will be credited to his Dividend Reinvestment account. Any participant who wishes to exercise stock purchase rights must request that stock certificates be sent him by Bradford as provided in Item 4, prior to the record date of the rights offering.

10. Neither Bradford nor its nominee or nominees shall have any responsibility beyond the exercise of ordinary care for any action taken or omitted pursuant to this Agreement nor shall they have any duties, responsibilities or liabilities except such as are expressly set forth herein. Neither shall they be liable hereunder for any act

Bradford Trust Company (continued)

done in good faith or for any good faith omission to act, including, without limitation, failure to terminate a participant's account prior to receipt of written notice of his death or with respect to the timing or the price of any purchase.

11. The participant shall have no right to draw checks or drafts against his account or to give instructions to Bradford in respect to any shares or cash held therein except as expressly provided herein.

12. The participant agrees to notify Bradford promptly in writing of any change of address. Notices to the participant may be given by letter addressed to the participant at his last address of record with Bradford.

13. This Agreement may be amended or supplemented by Bradford at any time or times by mailing appropriate notice at least 30 days prior to the effective date thereof to the participant at his last address of record. The amendment or supplement shall conclusively be deemed to be accepted by the participant unless prior to the effective date thereof Bradford receives written notice of the termination of his account. Any such amendment may include the appointment by Bradford in its place and stead of a successor agent under this Agreement provided such successor is a bank or trust company organized under the laws of the United States or any state thereof. [The company] is authorized to pay to such successor agent for the account of each participant in the Dividend Reinvestment Plan all dividends and distributions payable on shares of [the company's] Common Stock in his name or in his account, the same to be applied by such successor agent as provided in this Agreement.

14. This Agreement and the Enrollment Card signed by the participant (which is deemed a part of this Agreement) and participant's account shall be governed by and construed in accordance with the laws of the State of New York and the Rules of the Securities and Exchange Commission. The Agreement cannot be changed orally.

dividends at all. We are required by SEC regulations to allow participants to withdraw from the plan and receive their dividends if they notify us of their intention within ten days of the dividend payment date. Since we mail plan participants a quarterly report without a check on the payment date, we do catch most of these accounts (inadvertent enrollers) in time to make corrections."

Communication Lapses

Communication breakdowns are not confined to those encountered in conveying the terms and conditions for plan participation to investors. Others include: inaccurate informational exchanges between reinvestment administrators and transfer agents when these are separate organizations; failures of agents to respond fully to members' inquiries; and delays in providing plan members with status reports on their accounts.

Several respondents that employ different banks to serve as their dividend reinvestment and transfer agents indicate problems sometimes appear when transfer agents are slow or inaccurate in providing details on share ownership changes to the reinvestment agents or, conversely, when administrators dally in applying this information. To correct situations of this nature plan sponsors insist that their representatives establish closer working relationships. Pressure applied to both parties usually closes the communication gap.

"Our biggest problem in my estimation is that our stockholders, when writing to the bank regarding their accounts, do not receive the same attention to their gripes the company would give them," complains the vice president and secretary of a food company. A number of participants share this view. And to compensate for what they consider less than complete bank responsiveness to members' correspondence, a number interject themselves into the communication process. Some companies, instead of forwarding all plan-related inquiries to administrators for handling, become directly involved because they feel obliged to resolve the questions completely even though it means extra work. Other companies monitor informational exchanges between administrators and plan members.

Tardiness by administrators in advising plan members on the reinvestment of dividends or cash contributions bothers some sponsors. These delays, which sometimes relate to misunderstandings by participants of program provisions that ban the investment

Administrators' Perspectives on Problems

Banks that offer dividend reinvestment services acknowledge the existence of a few administrative difficulties. Proxy problems of one kind or another cause them some concern. So do unexpected changes in the record-keeping formats of transfer agents which occasionally result in the submission of data tapes that are incompatible with their existing systems. But banks are alert to these menaces and take countermeasures to control them.

Most other problems encountered are considered irritants — withdrawal notices received after dividends have been reinvested or requests for new stock certificates, for example. Bankers interviewed claim that mistakes regarding the crediting of dividends are precluded by their systems which provide for complete cash reconciliations and other checks prior to the reinvestment of accumulated members' funds.

"There were — and still are — occasional complaints due to administrative breakdowns in the handling of an account, misunderstandings about the terms of the plan, or a desire for a plan which is more tailored to the shareowner's personal investment needs." This statement by a utility executive whose company manages its own reinvestment program makes it clear that management problems are not confined to externally administered plans. Indeed, no participating concern that self-administers its reinvestment plan claims internal management provides a panacea.

of cash contributions until at least one dividend is reinvested, are usually eliminated within months of a plan's commencement. Sponsors demand timely service for investors; administrators respond by ironing out the wrinkles in their systems.

Another communication problem that springs up from time to time involves requests for proxies. But unlike the already discussed proxy-authorization card confusion, this difficulty traces to the receipt of two proxies — one covering shares held prior to enrollment and the other shares held in administrators' names — by plan participants. Sometimes, thinking the proxy received last is a duplicate sent in error, stockholders become annoyed and ignore it. To help eliminate this problem sponsors and administrators coordinate mailings to have proxies arrive at about the same time. And to provide a further indication that the requests are distinct the proxy forwarded by administrators refers to the precise number of shares (including fractions) held in custody — a total that almost invariably differs from that in the proxy sent by companies themselves.

Recordkeeping Errors

Problems involving duplicate accounts, incorrect dividend applications, and similar blunders rarely surface. But, when they do, sponsors require their administrators to take corrective actions, such as improving the quality of their computer programs or the caliber of their personnel. One, a mining company, has even set minimum acceptable performance standards with regard to record keeping for its administrator.

Broker Complaints

After instituting reinvestment programs, two participating companies became aware of grumblings from members of the brokerage community. Brokers complained their businesses were suffering as a result of commissions being diverted through plan memberships. The companies explained to the brokers that since most plan participants are small investors, who represent insignificant commission sources, their reinvestment programs do not pose competitive threats.

5.
Looking Forward

WITH A FEW EXCEPTIONS, reinvestment sponsors are sanguine about the future of these programs. For some, the past is merely prologue; they expect bigger and better things from plans that are already operating successfully. For others, the ongoing development of the reinvestment idea offers new opportunities; less than fully satisfied with their existing plans' accomplishments, they expect to introduce modifications to improve results.

Growth Prospects

Most of those queried look for increases in the number of companies sponsoring dividend reinvestment programs or in the number of stockholders participating in these programs, or both. Among the developments expected to spur this growth are: greater awareness by both corporations and individual investors of the advantages offered by reinvestment plans; reductions in the charges assessed plan members; and revisions in plan features to make them more attractive to sponsors and investors. Here are some typical comments:

"We believe that dividend reinvestment has a good future. We foresee the possible expansion of the limits on additional cash contributions, the possible expansion of the program to include the reinvestment in common stock of preferred stock dividends, and the possibility of discounts on the purchase price of common stock being offered to all participants. With these increased services, we would expect increased participation from our shareholders."

— *Manager of financial administration, a utility*

* * *

"I believe such programs will continue to grow for the following reasons:

"(1) They represent an inexpensive way for small, individual shareholders to acquire more shares of major corporations, especially since most plans include a voluntary feature allowing investment of funds in addition to cash dividend received.

those of high cash dividend paying companies such as utilities. In addition, it would provide equitable tax treatment to investors in high cash dividend paying companies and those in companies paying no dividends, low cash dividends, or only stock dividends. The increased equity investment induced by the change in the tax law would strengthen the capital structure of American industry and provide a base for increased capital expenditures and employment. The resulting stimulus to the economy provided by the increased reinvestment of common dividends would produce offsetting long-term tax revenues."

Format and Administrative Changes

While some respondents believe that, because of pressures from stockbrokers and the SEC, further changes in the form of dividend reinvestment programs are unlikely in the years immediately ahead, most of those offering opinions expect important modifications in the organization and management of many plans. Among the trends this group sees developing — some of which influence growth predictions — are:

- Expanding use of original shares to fill reinvestment demand
- Increasing absorption of costs by plan sponsors
- Increasing internal administration of plans
- Higher ceilings on supplementary cash contributions
- Discounting of prices on shares acquired through reinvestment of dividends
- Paying interest on cash contributions held for reinvestment.

Sixteen companies think that more and more reinvestment programs will utilize original shares to fill reinvestment demand. While most of these are capital-intensive utilities, several manufacturers see considerable merit in the approach. The principal advantage original share plans hold over other arrangements lies in their equity raising possibilities, as suggested earlier.

Raising capital through reinvestment programs may also prove less expensive than through formal underwritings. A recent newspaper article, for example, refers to the experience of a utility.[1] In the three or so years of its existence the company's

[1] Donald Saltz, "Dividend Reinvesting Rising Capital Source," *The Washington Star,* February 8, 1976.

original share plan has raised $9.3 million in equity capital at a cost of $210,000. This financing burden of just over two percent (the company absorbs administrative charges) compares favorably with the greater than five percent spread required to compensate investment bankers for the concern's most recent public stock offering.

Ten of those polled expect more program sponsors to assume some or all of the administrative charges now passed on to individual members. The treasurer of a chemical company contemplating such a move comments on its rationale and expected impact:

> "The program will probably be liberalized slightly in the future to the point where the company will offer to absorb all costs of the program. This will probably have the effect of further increasing the trend toward greater participation. Such participation might tend to provide a measure of greater stability in the pricing of the company's stock."

Six sponsors anticipate that an increasing number of companies will undertake administration of their own programs not only to seize cost saving opportunities but also to improve responsiveness to investors' needs. They feel additional moves in this direction will initially be concentrated among companies that maintain their own stockholder records and that possess the requisite computer capability.

Some respondents believe raising existing limits on voluntary cash contributions will encourage additional participation. Others think that allowing plan members to acquire new shares at a discount from market, such as the five percent price reduction now offered by one participating company on stock purchased with reinvested dividends, will facilitate corporate financing. And still others hold that providing returns on voluntary contributions awaiting reinvestment will encourage investors to make supplementary cash payments.

Appendix

The Reinvestment Program of General Telephone & Electronics Corporation

GENERAL TELEPHONE & Electronics Corporation (GTE), a large company which conducts significant telephone and manufacturing operations through more than 60 subsidiaries, established its original dividend reinvestment program in 1972. A bank reinvested dividends on behalf of participants in company shares purchased in the open market. Plan members paid service charges and proportionate shares of brokerage commissions to the bank.

In 1973, the program was expanded to permit the option of investing through voluntary cash contributions, and charges assessed members by the bank were reduced. Further modifications were made in 1975, and the present arrangement – called the Shareholder Systematic Investment Plan – provides for the issuance of original shares to fill reinvestment demand, and the absorption of all plan-related costs by the company. Responsibility for the management of this revised reinvestment program was assigned to GTE Shareholder Services Incorporated, a wholly owned subsidiary of GTE, which replaced the bank as administrator.

Any GTE common or preferred stockholder can participate in the GTE Shareholder Systematic Investment Plan. Stockholders may, as plan members, exercise any of these options: (1) have cash dividends from their common or preferred holdings automatically reinvested in common shares of GTE; or (2) reinvest their dividends, and also make quarterly optional cash payments of not less than $25 nor more than $3,000; or (3) make quarterly optional cash payments, within the same range, but continue to receive dividends in cash for shares registered in their names.

Through the forerunners of its current plan, GTE hoped to provide a convenient, systematic and inexpensive investment vehicle for shareholders, to increase shareholder loyalty, and to obtain a measure of market support for the common stock. In addition, with the introduction of the revised plan in 1975, the company anticipated not only an increase in shareholder participation but also an expansion of the stockholder base. Moreover, it expected the plan to provide a continuing and increasing source of equity capital.

GTE SHAREHOLDER SYSTEMATIC INVESTMENT PLAN

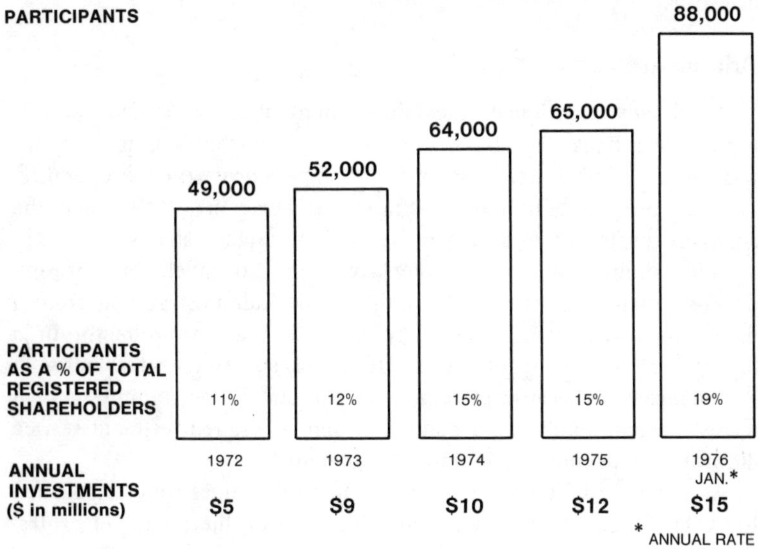

Degree of Success

GTE is pleased with the favorable reception accorded its plan; participation has exceeded original expectations. As the accompanying chart from the company's 1975 annual report shows, membership has increased at an annual rate of nearly 16 percent since the plan's inception in 1972. At the outset of 1976, over 19 percent of all registered GTE shareholders were participating, investing at the rate of about $15 million annually. Seventy-four percent of the approximately 88 thousand participants own 100 shares or less of company stock.

Management advances five main reasons for the growing participation in the company's reinvestment plan. These are:

- Addition of a cash investment option;
- Reduction and eventual elimination of service charges;
- Resolicitation of all shareholders when the present plan was launched;
- Dissemination of information about the plan in the annual report, at shareholder meetings, and during other contacts with shareholders; and

• Recognition of the plan's benefits by an increasing number of investors.

Administration

As already mentioned, the reinvestment plan was initially administered by a bank. The bank served as the company's transfer agent, was familiar with its records, and had experience with the operation of such programs. In-house management began in 1975, when the company shifted to an arrangement utilizing original shares.

Self-administration was undertaken not so much out of any dissatisfaction with the work of the former administrator as from a desire to manage an increasingly important activity directly in a highly customized manner. Cost, too, was something of a factor in the changeover. Because the company was already performing its own record keeping, adding the administration of the reinvestment service did not require substantial staff enlargement.

At the time of conversion, three major guidelines were established for GTE Shareholder Services in administering the plan: (1) professional management in accordance with the terms and conditions set forth in the prospectus describing the plan; (2) expeditious processing of statements detailing the status of each member's account; and (3) prompt, courteous and accurate handling of correspondence and all other relationships with shareowners. Since taking over the plan's management, that subsidiary has been very successful in meeting the established guidelines, and it continuously analyzes various methods of improving the service to GTE shareholders.